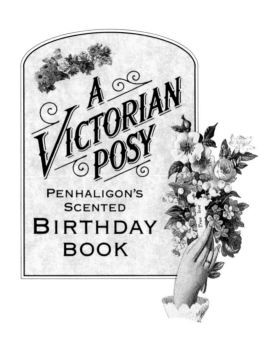

A Victorian Posy

PENHALIGON'S SCENTED

BIRTHDAY BOOK

THIS BOOK BELONGS TO

⚜ INTRODUCTION ⚜

R<small>AISE</small> me a daïs of silk and down;
   Hang it with vair and purple dyes;
Carve it in doves and pomegranates,
   And peacocks with a hundred eyes;
Work it in gold and silver grapes,
   In leaves and silver fleurs-de-lys;
Because the birthday of my life
   Is come, my love is come to me.

A BIRTHDAY. CHRISTINA GEORGINA ROSSETTI, 1830-1894

Dear Friend,

Christina Rossetti would undoubtedly have recorded
the date on which she wrote this verse over one
hundred years ago in her Birthday Book. For a
Birthday Book may be used not only to record the
birthdays of those we hold dear, but other significant
dates too: births, deaths, a meeting with a loved one.
And especially anniversaries! The traditional wedding
anniversaries, Silver, Ruby, Gold and even Paper may
be recorded here, and what better gift from a friend
than the remembrance of a special day.

   As you turn the leaves, I hope you will enjoy the
scent of Victorian Posy which perfumes the endpapers.
This most evocative of all our senses will take us back
to memories of festive days gone by, of which I hope
this small book may serve as a reminder.

Sheila Pickles, London 1990

— JANUARY —

1

2

3

4

5

6

7

8

9

10

11

12

13

14

15

16

17

18

19

20

21

Jack Frost was in the garden;
    I saw him there at dawn;
He was dancing round the bushes
    And prancing on the lawn.
He had a cloak of silver,
    A hat all shimm'ring white,
A wand of glittering star-dust,
    And shoes of sunbeam light.

JOHN P. SMEETON, 19th CENTURY

22

23

24

25

26

27

28

29

30

31

THEN came your violets—and at once I heard
  The sparrows chatter on the dripping eaves,
The full stream's babbling inarticulate word,
The plash of rain on big wet ivy-leaves;
I saw the woods where thick the dead leaves lie,
And smelt the fresh earth's scent—the scent of memory.

EDITH NESBIT, 1858-1924

— FEBRUARY —

1

2

3

4

5

6

7

8

9

10

11

12

13

14

15

16

17

You ask why Spring's fair first-born flower is white :
  Peering from out the warm earth long ago,
It saw above its head great drifts of snow,
  And blanched with fright.

CLINTON SCOLLARD, 19th CENTURY

18

19

20

21

22

23

24

25

26

27

28

29

MARCH

1
....

2
....

3

4

5

6

7

8

9

10

11

12

13

14

15

16

17

18

19

20

SUCH a commotion under the ground,
    When March called, "Ho there! ho!"
Such spreading of rootlets far and wide,
    Such whisperings to and fro!
"Are you ready?" the Snowdrop asked,
    " 'Tis time to start, you know."
"Almost, my dear!" the Scilla replied,
    "I'll follow as soon as you go."
Then "Ha! ha! ha!" a chorus came
    Of laughter sweet and low,
From millions of flowers under the ground,
    Yes, millions beginning to grow.

RALPH W. EMERSON, 1803-1882

21

22

23

24

25

26

27

28

29

30

31

APRIL

1
....

2
....

3

4

5

6

7

8

9

10

11

Of all the months that fill the year,
Give April's month to me,
For earth and sky are then so filled
With sweet variety.

LETITIA E. LANDON, 1802-1838

12

13

14

15

16

17

18

19

Buttercups and daisies,
  Oh, the pretty flowers;
Coming ere the spring-time,
  To tell of sunny hours,
While the trees are leafless,
  While the fields are bare,
Buttercups and daisies
  Spring up here and there.

MARY HOWITT, 19th CENTURY

20

21

22

23

24

25

26

27

28

29

30

MAY

1

2

3

4

5

6

7

8

9

10

11

12

13

14

Hail! fairy queen, adorned with flowers,
   Attended by the smiling hours,
'Tis thine to dress the rosy bowers
      In colours gay;
We love to wander in thy train,
To meet thee on the fertile plain
To bless thy soft propitious reign,
      O lovely May!

MRS. HEMANS, 1793-1835

15

16

MAY

17

....

18

....

19

....

20

....

21

....

22

....

23

....

24

25

26

27

28

29

30

31

JUNE

1
....

2
....

3
....

....

4

5

6

7

8

9

10

11

12

THERE is nothing held so dear
      As love, if only it be hard to win.
The roses that in yonder hedge appear
      Outdo our garden-buds which bloom within ;
But since the hand may pluck them every day,
Unmarked they bud, bloom, drop, and drift away.

JEAN INGELOW, 1820-1897

13

14

15

16

17

18

19

20

21

22

23

24

25

26

27

28

29

30

JULY

1 ....

2 ....

....

⟶✖ JULY ✖⟵

3

4

5

6

7

8

9

10

11

Fairy places, fairy things,
  Fairy woods where the wild bee wings,
Tiny trees for tiny dames—
These must all be fairy names!

ROBERT LOUIS STEVENSON, 1850-1894

12

13

14

15

16

17

18

19

20

21

22

23

24

25

26

27

28

29

30

31

AUGUST

1 ....

2 ....

3 ....

4

5

6

7

8

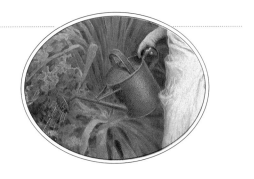

9

10

11

12

13

14

15

16

Love's language may be talked with these;
To work out choicest sentences
No blossoms can be meeter;
And, such being used in Eastern bowers,
Young maids may wonder if the flowers
Or meanings be the sweeter.

ELIZABETH BARRETT BROWNING, 1806-1861

17

18

19

20

21

22

23

24

25

26

27

28

29

30

31

SEPTEMBER

1

2

3

❧ SEPTEMBER ❧

4

5

6

7

8

9

10

11

12

Flower in the crannied wall
I pluck you out of the crannies
I hold you here, root and all, in my hand
Little flower—but if I could understand
What you are, root and all, and all in all
I should know what God and man is.

ALFRED TENNYSON, 1809-1892

13

14

15

16

17

18

19

20

21

22

23

24

25

26

27

28

Wɪᴛʜ locks of gold to-day ;
To-morrow, silver grey ;
Then blossom-bald. Behold,
O man, thy fortune told !

Jᴏʜɴ B. Tᴀʙʙ, 19th ᴄᴇɴᴛᴜʀʏ

29

30

October

1

2

3

4

5

6

7

8

9

10

11

12

13

14

15

16

17

....

18

....

19

....

20

....

21

....

G OD made a little gentian;
    It tried to be a rose
And failed, and all the summer laughed.
    But just before the snows
There came a purple creature
    That ravished all the hill;
And summer hid her forehead,
    And mockery was still.
The frosts were her condition;
    The Tyrian would not come
Until the North evoked it,
    "Creator! shall I bloom?"

EMILY DICKINSON, 1830-1886

22

23

24

25

26

27

28

29

30

31

—NOVEMBER—

1

....

2

....

3

....

4

5

6

7

8

9

10

11

12

13

Go, sit upon the lofty hill,
    And turn your eyes around,
Where waving woods and waters wild
    Do hymn an autumn sound.
The summer sun is faint on them—
    The summer flowers depart—
Sit still—as all transformed to stone,
    Except your musing heart.

ELIZABETH BARRETT BROWNING, 1806-1861

14

15

16

17

18

19

20

21

22

23

24

25

26

27

28

29

30

—DECEMBER—

1

2

3

4

5

6

7

8

9

10

11

12

13

14

15

16

17

18

19

20

21

22

23

24

~ DECEMBER ~

25

26

27

28

29

30

31

ACKNOWLEDGEMENTS

The majority of the illustrations were supplied by
Fine Art Photographic Library. Additional material from:
Bridgeman Art Library; Richard Hagen Gallery, Worcestershire;
Limpsfield Watercolours, Limpsfield, Surrey;
Royal Botanic Gardens at Kew; Royal Horticultural Society.

Front cover: *Leisure Moments*, E. Walbourn/Fine Art
Photographic Library
Back cover: © Penhaligon's Limited 1979

PENHALIGON'S VICTORIAN POSY

The Victorian Posy range of perfumes and scented
gifts was created by Penhaligon's for an exhibition entitled
"The Garden" at the Victoria and Albert Museum in 1979.
It is the most English of scents for it contains only English
country garden flowers, and has the scent of a true
Victorian posy. Following its success, it seemed natural to
complement the perfume with a series of books, sweetly
scented and reflecting the floral theme.
If you would like more information on the Victorian Posy range
of products, or on Penhaligon's other ranges of perfumes
and gifts, please telephone 01-836 2150. Alternatively, please
visit one of Penhaligon's shops at:

41 Wellington Street, Covent Garden, London WC2
55 Burlington Arcade, Piccadilly, London W1
20a Brook Street, Mayfair, London W1
69 Moorgate, City, London EC2
12 Northumberland Place, Bath, Avon
36 Stonegate, York
22 Eastgate Row, Chester

Published by
HARMONY Books, a division of Crown Publishers, Inc.,
201 East 50th Street, New York, New York 10022

Published in Great Britain by
Pavilion Books Limited, London in 1990

HARMONY and colophon are trademarks of Crown Publishers, Inc.

Made and printed in Portugal by Printer Portuguesa

A LOC number for this book is available from the Library of Congress

ISBN 0-517-57854-9

10 9 8 7 6 5

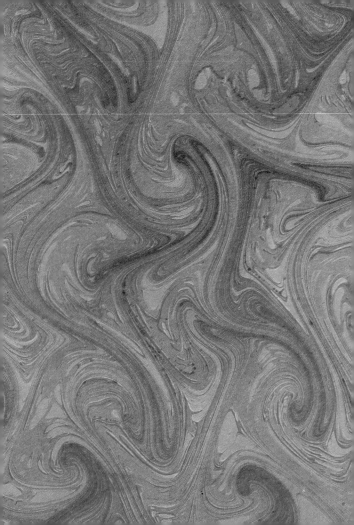